HAPPINESS

BY

THOMAS ALEXANDER

Happiness by Thomas Alexander

Direct Light Publications
45 Dudley Court, Endell Street, London, WC2H 9RF

Permissions may be sought directly from Publishing Rights Department 45 Dudley Court, Endell Street, London, WC2H 9RF
performance@directlight-publications.com

Library of Congress Cataloguing in Publication Data
Application submitted.
British Library Cataloguing in Publication Data
Application submitted.
03 04 05 06 07 08 10 9 8 7 6 5 4 3
ISBN 978-1-941979-12-9

–

Edited by Shirin Laghai for Direct Light Publications.

Cover Design by SimplyA

HAPPINESS

Synopsis

ON A REMOTE HEADLAND IN NORTH WALES A MAN AND HIS PARAPLEGIC SON DREAM OF LIFE BEYOND THE CONFINES OF THEIR FOUR WALLS.

BUT WHEN A WOMAN OFFERS THEM THE ESCAPE THEY SO CRAVE, THEY FIND THEY ARE BOUND BY MORE THAN THEIR DREAMS.

THE JEALOUSY OF A BORED POLICEMAN AND THE KINDNESS OF A MAIL-ORDER BRIDE SET THEM ON A PATH OF HOPE AND DESTRUCTION.

ABOUT THE AUTHOR

Thomas Alexander has worked in almost all forms of theatre, from opera to children's performances, working as everything from stage hand to costume designer, and has seen his work translated into four different languages and performed as far afield as America and Afghanistan.

His complete plays, along with his first novel, A *Scattering Of Orphans,* have been published by Direct Light Publications.

Also by the Author

PLAYS

Happiness
Murder Me Gently
The Family
Begat
The Crossroads Country
Great
The Visitor
When Dusk Brings Glory
The Recruitment Officer
Writer's Block
The Last Christmas
Writing William
The Big Match

ONE ACT PLAYS

Four Widows and A Funeral
For Arts Sake
The TV
Life TM
The Dance
The Pink Cow

ADAPTATIONS

William Shakespeare's' R3
Othello

NOVELS

A Scattering Of Orphans

FOREWORD

You are not allowed to take photos of the grave of Alexander Litvinenko. Under orders from his wife, the tour guides in the cemetery north of London where he has been laid to rest, standing near the graves of such luminaries as Karl Marx and Douglas Adams, ask visitors not to take snaps, but they pause, nonetheless and ask tourists from the USA, Europe, et al, if they know who the man is before regaling them with the story of one of the strangest assassinations of the last century.

But no one tells the story of Anna Politkovskaya, Vyacheslav Yaroshenko, Magomed Yevloyev, Telman Alishayav, and the many other journalists and lawyers assassinated for speaking out about the practices of the Russian government.

I began writing Murder Me Gently during the rehearsal period for the Tokyo production of The Crossroads Country in 2009 following the assassination of human rights lawyers Stanislv Markelov and Annastasia Baburova on a Moscow Street. I'd known for some time that I wanted to write about state sovereignty and corporate interests under the guise of some sort of comedy, and as sad as this was it seemed like the perfect opportunity. Like many others, I had been following the progression of Russia under Vladimir Putin into a totalitarian oligarchy with interest, and the assassinations, together with the invasion of Georgia by Russian troops in 2008, convinced me that there was something intrinsically incredulous that needed to be told.

The more I researched, the more I found the world of modern Russian international relations bizarre. From Litzinenko and the strange case of MV Artic Sea – current during the first draft and seemingly boarded and pirated by members of Mossad to prevent its real cargo from reaching Syria – to Vladimir Putin's election to Prime Minister and the installation of the puppet (and, importantly, hirsute) Dmitry Medvedev as President. All of these events seemed more out of the pen of John Le Carre or Graham Green, or even – increasingly – Raymond Chandler than Pravda or The New York Times.

The more outlandish the plots, it appeared, the more likely that they could be true. When Litvinenko and his followers claimed that he had been poisoned by the Russian government with close ties to the mafia the West let out a stifled guffaw, but within months it became clear that this was indeed the case. The invasion of Georgia and the subsequent withdrawal seemed at first to be a case of the right hand not knowing what the left was doing, but quickly became understood as a strategic masterstroke (and one which would be repeated in the Ukraine in 2014).

Russia's approach to world politics and media criticism seemed a plot so ridiculous in nature that it could have been filmed by Howard Hawks, who infamously stated when asked about the plot of The Big Sleep: "Don't ask me, I'm just the director!"

I love Film Noir. It's incredibly fun to write, and I have always been drawn to the kind of failed anti-heroes and destructive personas that populate the genre. It's also not something you often see on stage. Coming into production in Tokyo in 2009 we were broke, and

I knew that I needed something that would work well on a black box stage with minimal props and costumes. That, together with the outlandish acts of the FSB and their close ties with Putin, convinced me that this was the best way to illuminate Russia's human rights abuses and international conflicts, a belief which only increased by the time the play was eventually put on.

Murder Me Gently finally saw production in Cambridge 2011, with a limited run ending in London in 2012. During that time the arrest of Pussy Riot, the assassination of Natalia Estemirova, and beating of Sapiyat Magomedova, amongst many other events, had all caught the world's attention.

Since then, Russia has continued to act globally without impunity, invading the Ukraine in 2013, funding Syria, and banning homosexuals from the Sochi winter Olympics of 2014 when "enforcers" were sent out around the Olympic Village with horsewhips to beat protestors.

I'd like to make a joke about Howard Hawks, but I can't. I'd like to say the West is better, but Edward Snowdon is currently living as an asylum seeker in Moscow. The plot has become too preposterous.

Thomas Alexander – 2014

Cast of Characters

No of cast: 6

Gregori Harrison	Fifties. Male. Rough. Imposing.
Sarah Cranshaw	Early Thirties. Female. Besuited. Attractive.
Gareth Harrison	Thirties. Male. Paraplegic. Slight.
Stan	Thirties. Male. Tall. Strong.
Angel	Late Thirties. Female. Thai. Faded beauty.
Police	Forties / Fifties. Male. Bitter

HAPPINESS

Happiness was originally performed in London in 2010.

Produced by Crossroads Theatre Company, it was directed by Alec Harris.

ORIGINAL CAST

Gregori Harrison	Alan Hays
Sarah Cranshaw	Genevieve Cleghorn
Gareth Harrison	Alec Harris
Stan	Declan Lynch
Angel	Helene Salvini-Fujita
Police	Howard Corlett

HAPPINESS

ACT 1

ACT 1

SCENE 1

A HOUSE ON THE EAST COAST OF NORTH WALES – NO TIME.

WHETHER STAGED IN TWO STORIES OR ONE, THE HOUSE IS DIVIDED INTO TWO SEPARATE AREAS, A KITCHEN WITH A FRONT DOOR AND A BEDROOM.

THE HOUSE, SPARTAN AND BADLY KEPT IS CLEARLY LIVED IN ONLY BY MEN. DISHES LIE UNKEMPT IN THE SINK. FOOD LEFT TO ROT ON THE TABLE.

IN THE BEDROOM, A GOOD SIZED BED SITS CENTRE. A MAN, GARETH, DWARFED IN IT.

AMONGST OTHER THINGS THE ROOM CONTAINS A CHAIR BY THE SIDE OF THE BED, A DESK WITH A PITCHER OF WATER ON IT, A GRAMOPHONE/RECORD PLAYER, A DRESSING MIRROR, AND A HAT-STAND WHICH HOLDS THE KIND OF COAT THE CAPTAIN OF A FISHING TRAWLER MIGHT WEAR.

ALTHOUGH THE HOUSE LOOKS NORMAL TO THE EYE, A CHANGE OF LIGHTING SHOULD TRANSFORM IT INTO THE DECK OF A SHIP COMPLETE WITH MAST, PLANK, AND PROW.

THIS IS THE SHIP OF DREAMS WHERE THE BODY OF GARETH, A QUADRIPLEGIC, DREAMS OF ESCAPE AND ANOTHER LIFE.

ROPES, THAT SEEM ORNAMENTAL WHEN WE ARE WATCHING THE HOUSE, HANG ABOVE EITHER SIDE OF THE SHIP.

CURTAINS ON THE SHIP, GARETH STANDING CENTRE STAGE, LOOKING OUT FROM THE PROW OF THE SHIP.

BEHIND HIM THE LIGHTS FADE AND FLICKER, REVEALING THE HOUSE. A WOMAN, HIS MOTHER, PLAYED BY THE SAME ACTRESS AS SARAH, CROSSES THE KITCHEN BUSYING HERSELF WITH SOUP.

SHE MOVES THROUGH THE KITCHEN INTO THE BEDROOM, CARRYING A TRAY.

AS SHE DOES SO A MAN, GREG, MOVES MENACINGLY UNSEEN UP BEHIND GARETH.

HE WRAPS A ROPE AROUND GARETH'S NECK AND DRAGS HIM BACK AT THE SAME TIME AS THE 'MOTHER' REACHES THE PLANK AND WRAPS A NOOSE AROUND HER OWN NECK.

GARETH IS PULLED BACK 'INTO' THE HOUSE AS THE LIGHTS OF THE BOAT FADE AND LEFT FOR DEAD ON THE BED AT THE EXACT SAME TIME AS THE 'MOTHER' JUMPS TO HER DEATH.

WE FADE TO BLACK, LEAVING A MOMENTARY SPOT ON THE HANGING 'MOTHER' BEFORE IT TOO FADES, LEAVING A BUTTERFLY IN IT'S PLACE, FLYING ABOVE THE STAGE. FINALLY IT ALSO DISAPPEARS INTO THE BLACKNESS.

THE IMAGE IS PROFOUND, SCARY, AND VERY REALISTIC.

SCENE 2

GARETH IS SITTING IN BED, DEBUSSY'S 'FOOTPRINTS IN THE SNOW' PLAYING ON THE GRAMOPHONE. HE IS WRITING, THE PENCIL ATTACHED TO THE STICK IN HIS MOUTH HE MOVES IT ALONG THE PAPER TO HIS RIGHT.

THE RECORD IS SCRATCHED AND STICKS. GARETH TRIES TO IGNORE IT BUT HE CANNOT WRITE WITH THE DISTRACTION AND SPITS THE STICK OUT INCREASINGLY ANNOYED.

GREG ENTERS THE KITCHEN AND HEARING THE MUSIC, MOVES THROUGH TO THE BEDROOM, RELUCTANTLY.

NEITHER MAN SPEAKS UNTIL GREG REACHES THE GRAMOPHONE AND TURNS IT OFF.

GREG   How's it going?

GARETH   You're late.

GREG   There was talk at the cannery, like. Laying more people off. Spill and everything I suppose…

GARETH   Started without you.

GREG   (STOPS, TIRED) Right. Sure?

GARETH   Smell it, munn.

GREG   Right. Lets have a look then.

GREG COMES TO THE BED AND TAKES THE STICK BEFORE TURNING GARETH ON HIS SIDE.

GARETH   Didn't wanna wait for you. Not that I tried to stop him, yeah. Couldn't stop him, if I'd wanted to. Seemed pretty set on it.

GREG   You writing?

GARETH   A good one, I think. About a father who can't control his son: apocryphal.

GREG   (EXASPERATED) Aww... How'd it come off again.

GARETH   Maybe he did it!? He's a malicious little fucker. A fucking bastard if you're asking my opinion.

GREG   You know I don't like it when you talk like that.

GARETH   It's rubber, man; perishable. Everything perishes. That's the moral of the story. The da, the one who has the son he can't control: perishes. Perishes in a fire. Takes both of them with it. Father and son. Whoosh – and it's all over. The father and the uncontrollable son. One big out of control fire and they die; both of them. Controlled at last. Just not by each other.

GREG   I'll need the pan.

EXIT GREG.

GARETH   The da dies first yeah? Smoke! Smoke rises, even with generations. Can't feel it of course, nice and peaceful, one long sleep after another. The son though... Feels everything... Cursed by an unnatural speech pattern. (CALLING AFTER HIM) He never respected you, you know? Never respected me neither. Wouldn't be surprised if he just popped the thing off and inertia be damned. (SOTTO) That's what I'd have fucking done. (CALLING ONCE MORE) I'm not my brother's keeper, you know!

5

(PAUSE) What happened at the cannery? (PAUSE) Da? (PAUSE) What happened at the cannery?

ENTER GREG HOLDING A PAN AND PROCEEDING TO CLEAN.

GREG   (REPEATING RHETORIC) People aren't eating fish, right; spills, imports… They're laying people off.

GARETH   But not you though.

GREG   Yeah, not me. Stan though. You remember Stan?

GARETH   (SNIDE) Fuck's that supposed to mean?

GREG   Now, there's no need for that, is there.

GARETH   Do I remember him? Fuck do you think?

GREG   Last one in, first one out. That's what they said. I don't know. Feel bad about it though, you know what I mean?

GARETH   Stan's a big boy. A very large boy-man when you come to think about it.

GREG   He'd just got settled as well. Started to make a go of it?! They had him on the paper line. Simple enough. Twist and turn, nothing more, and all the boys like him.

GARETH   He'll bounce back.

GREG   Easy for you to say.

GARETH   Boy's built to bounce.

GREG   They were offering ship jobs; but he ain't got the experience. Can't have him on the deck. No coordination.

GARETH   (WORRIED) They're offering ship jobs?

GREG   For those they lay off, like.

GARETH   I was thinking about putting him on ship. The boy. I was thinking about… I don't know… he goes off in search of himself. On a boat. One of the ones you used to work on, like? He goes off in search of himself and well; I'm thinking of drowning him. On the boat. But maybe not. Maybe… he finds something, I mean, I don't want it to be too Moby Dick, or Hemingway or whatever, but he finds something, something he brings back to the mainland. For his da. I don't know.

GREG   A new catheter'd be an idea.

GARETH   Fuck's he gonna find a new catheter at sea?

GREG   There, it's on again. Anyway, I was thinking I should have a word like. Stan. Go over to his place tonight. If that's not too much trouble. After supper, like.

GARETH   Aye, right.

GREG   I just thought I'd go over there. Talk to his mam. Make sure they're alright.

GARETH   I said alright, didn't I?

GREG   He might be in a bad way, that's all.

GARETH   Right. Might be bedbound!

GREG   I'll get you your dinner first.

GARETH   No. I'm not hungry.

GREG   Now! You got to eat.

GARETH   Ah, he does. Not me. I get the messages, that's all. I don't give a fuck one way or the other. I just get the messages. He tells me to tell you he's hungry, he tells me to tell you he's pissed, and right now he's telling me to tell you he's fucked if he's going to have more of your fucking soup!

GREG   (FINISHED, WEARY) Tell him I'm going out then. Sheets are wet. I'll turn him when I get back.

GARETH   I'll let him know.

GREG   You do that.

GREG TURNS TO GO.

GARETH   Da! Da! Music man?!

GREG   Oh, right enough.

GARETH   I think it's scratched.

GREG TURNS OFF THE RECORD PLAYER.

GREG   We'll turn it off then, shall we?

GARETH   Define; we.

GREG   I'll be back to turn you in a few hours.

GARETH   Don't be surprised if we've gone out for a kebab.

EXIT GREG.

GARETH HUMS THE LAST FEW BARS OF THE MUSIC. HE LOOKS UP AT THE CLOTHES ON THE PEG.

GARETH   Fuck do you want?

LOOKING DOWN AT HIS BODY.

GARETH   (CONT.) Again? God you're a greedy little fucker aren't you? It's all me, me, me with you! Want to lock me up with someone more giving next time. Someone who, you know, will take the time to get to know me a little. Little give and take. We've been living together, how long? My mother warned me about people like you? Oh, yes, she did. Said you'd be the death of me, she did. Shows how little she knew.

You done? Excellent. Right down the tube this time? Good for you. Don't get me wrong or anything. You used to be one of my favourite people, but seriously, these days… You're pissing me off, if you pardon the pun. All you do is hold is me back,

GARETH FALLS ASLEEP.

AND HE ASLEEP RISES, PUTS ON THE SEA COAT AS…

LIGHTS UP ON THE SHIP OF DREAMS.

NOISE ACCOMPANIES THE TRANSFORMATION. GARETH ROCKS WITH IT, LISTING WITH THE BOAT HE'S ON.

HE GOES ACROSS AND PUTS ON THE RECORD AGAIN, WHICH THIS TIME PLAYS 'EROTICA IN E FLAT MAJOR'.

HIS FATHER ENTERS DRESSED AS IF ON A SHIP.

GREG   Captain!

GARETH HOLDS UP A FINGER AND CONDUCTS UNTIL IT REACHES CRESCENDO.

GREG   (CONT.) Captain!!!

GARETH   (CLIPPED ENGLISH TONES) Mr. Harrison, have I not told you to wait until spoken to?

GREG   But, Captain! It's the First Mate, sir!

GARETH   What is it this time?

GREG   He's dead.

GARETH   Really? Well, that is tricky!? What was it this time? Killer whale? Pirates? An inability to circumnavigate by the stars?

GREG   No, sir. Gout, sir.

GARETH   Gout?

GREG   Gout.

GARETH   Can gout kill?

GREG   The First Mate would reckon on it.

GARETH   Really, well that is unfortunate. Death by mutiny I can understand. Even death by drinking seawater, but gout? That's just undignified.

GREG   Yes, Captain.

GARETH   Well, that's an end to it. Better make him walk the plank.

GREG   Captain?

GARETH   The plank, Mr. Harrison. Make him walk it.

GREG   But he's dead.

GARETH   Still. It's good for moral.

GREG   Yes, Captain.

GARETH   Have we plotted a course?

GREG   Due south.

GARETH   I remember my First Mate. Knew there was a joke in there somewhere… Tell me, Mr. Harrison. You ever heard The Rime of the Ancient Mariner?

GREG   Can't say I have, no.

GARETH   There is absolutely nothing that rhymes with mariner. (SHRUGS) We have been to the ends of the earth, have we not, Mr. Harrison.

GREG   If you say so.

GARETH   We have been to the ends of the earth. Seen the sun rise off the Cape of Good Hope, seen it set in the seas of the eternal night. I'd like to go there again, Mr. Harrison. Once this; awkwardness with the First Mate's dealt with I'd like you to find a safe harbour and sail away from it. Do you understand?

GREG   Yes, Captain.

GARETH PICKS UP A KNIFE

GARETH   Oh, and Bosun.

GREG   Yes, Captain?

GARETH   (WELSH ACCENT) You let him die! You just let him lie there and die, didn't you! Didn't you! You just let him lie there and die!

HE STABS HIM, OVER AND OVER.

GARETH   All those years, you just let him lie there. All those years!!! You bastard! You fucking bastard!!! All those years!!!

FADE TO BLACK.

SCENE 3

THE HOUSE.

IT'S MORNING. GREG, DRESSED NORMALLY AGAIN, IS DRYING DISHES.

THERE'S A KNOCK ON THE DOOR AND HE GOES TO ANSWER.

ENTER SARAH.

SARAH   Hello. I'm looking for Mr. Harris?

GREG   Harrison, love.

SARAH   Mr. Harris?

GREG   Harrison. Trust me.

SARAH   You're Gregori Harri… Harrison?

GREG   How can I help?

SARAH   You have a Mr. Gareth Harris… Harrison, in your care.

GREG   That's right. My son.

SARAH   Can I come in? I'm from the Board of Welfare.

THERE'S A DISTINCT PAUSE AND THEN HE STANDS ASIDE. SARAH ENTERS, LOOKING AROUND, HIDING HER DISDAIN.

SARAH   There's just the two of you?

GREG   Me and the boy, right.

SARAH   And he lives here?

GREG   Where else?

SARAH   Yes, well, I'm from the Board of Welfare…

GREG   You said that.

SARAH   It's a long walk up here. With the hill and everything. From the town, I mean. You wouldn't happen to have a glass of water would you?

THERE IS SILENCE WHILE SHE IS POURED WATER.

SARAH   Thank you. As I was saying. I'm from the Board of Welfare and I've come to assess your situation with your son.

GREG   Alright.

SARAH   Is there anything he needs? Anything we can do for him?

GREG   Besides a new body?

SARAH   Well, yes.

GREG   He's fine.

SARAH   And there's just the two of you?

GREG   What can I do for you, Miss…

SARAH   Ms. – Cranshaw. Sarah. Please. Sarah.

GREG   I got a shift at eleven.

SARAH   Well, I wanted to talk about your son's situation.

GREG   Situation? He's quadriplegic, miss. He can't walk. Can't move. Anything. Soils the bed! Can't help it, yeah, not his fault, but that's the 'situation', right there. I turn him as often as I can, but he gets sores…

SARAH   Yes, of course.

GREG   So I don't know quite what you mean by his 'situation' if you catch my drift.

SARAH   (GESTURING TO SEAT) May I? (GREG SHRUGS) Your son's been like this for; what, ten years now? Am I right?

GREG   Twelve in August.

SARAH   That must be quite a strain; the two of you, up here alone.

GREG   We get by, like.

SARAH   You claim benefits.

GREG   We do what we can.

SARAH   From the government?

GREG   I work. In the cannery, like.

SARAH   But you claim benefits?

GREG   My son is locked in his bed, miss. I don't mean to be rude but he's locked in his bed. It's not the easiest of situations and… we claim benefits. We're entitled to benefits. There's just me and him and he's locked to his bed.

SARAH   I'm not doubting…

GREG   You're asking if we claim benefits. Yes, we claim benefits.

SARAH   Perhaps… I'm sorry… Perhaps… How did your son come to be in this situation, Mr. Harrison?

GREG   If there's a problem with the paperwork…

SARAH   I'm just… Perhaps if I understand the nature of the accident it would help us with your claim.

GREG   Claim? There's no claim. We've been on benefit for ten year! Even before his mother…

SARAH   No, no, of course not, I'm sorry. It's just… it's the word we use. It's… I misspoke. Every claim must be evaluated, that's all. Constantly. It's a matter of procedure. Nothing more.

GREG   Procedure.

SARAH   That's all.

GREG   Alright.

SARAH   The accident?

GREG   There's little to say. Car hit him off his bike and that was it.

SARAH   This was in Germany?

GREG   Germany. Düsseldorf.

SARAH   Where he was living?

GREG   That's right.

SARAH   And he'd never shown any signs of illness before?

GREG   Like what, the inability to hold his head up?

SARAH   I'm just asking.

GREG   No. He'd never shown any signs of… illness before. He was touring the world, for Christ's sake! Taken a year off before going to college and all that! He was, I don't know, he had friends there. (HE GETS UP AND GOES TO COLLECT A POSTCARD) People he'd met travelling. Australians. They visited here. After the accident. Flew all the way. Nice boys. One of them still sends postcards.

SARAH   And he was flown back here by the insurance company.

GREG   Well, eventually. I'm… Look, don't talk to me about that, alright? It took… He flew back. He flew back and now he's here. He's been here for twelve years! Twelve years in August! If there was a problem…

SARAH   There's no problem.

GREG   Alright then.

SARAH   These are just routine. We all have a job to do.

GREG   I'm gonna put the kettle on. You want some?

SARAH   I'm fine.

GREG BUSIES HIMSELF WITH THE KETTLE WHILE SHE TALKS.

SARAH   It's very important to us that people under our care are getting adequate care, the correct kind of care, you understand what I'm saying? I'm saying that we're here to help. I know it can often seem like we're the enemy but I can assure you we're not. The council is very eager to create dialogue not just with the patients but with their care givers, yeah? It's important to us that all needs are addressed in the correct way by the correct people. Money is not always the answer. You understand? For some people it's… an ear to talk to. A shoulder. Someone to help share the burden? It's… It must be very hard. On you. Looking after him for all these years.

GREG   It's what it is, innit?

SARAH   Of course. And he's your son. It's commendable. It truly is. A lot of people feel like that. They do. The sacrifice… Studies have shown however that just because people are with their families… this isn't always the best way for them to get care, you understand. Professionals…

GREG   He doesn't want to go into a home.

SARAH   No, of course not. No one wants that. No one wants to do exercise either but… What is it you do, Mr. Harrison?

GREG   I got a job at the cannery.

SARAH   You used to be a fisherman, am I right?

GREG   A longboat man, right.

SARAH   You took a job in the cannery..?

GREG   After his mother died.

SARAH   This was in..?

GREG   Four years ago.

SARAH   She died of a heart attack?

GREG   Right.

SARAH   So you took a job at the cannery to help your son?

GREG   He's got to be turned… If he's on one side for longer than three hours he gets sores…

SARAH   I understand. What I'm saying is; you made sacrifices. You made sacrifices for him. I'm guessing that working on a boat pays more?

GREG   It's not like there's much choice in the

matter, is there?

SARAH   No, that's what I'm saying. People think – families think that sacrifice, sacrificing themselves for their families is noble, and it is, but what I'm saying, what studies have shown, is that it might not always be the best way. For them. For the patient. (PAUSE) When was the last time a social worker visited you?

GREG   We get by.

SARAH   Of course, but the last time?

GREG   About eighteen months ago.

SARAH   You refused care.

GREG   Outside people… they remind him. Of things.

SARAH   He was suicidal.

GREG   He has his times, like.

SARAH   But he was suicidal. Eighteen months ago.

GREG   It's not like he can do anything about it, can he?

SARAH   But he was asking. In this letter. He was asking for assisted suicide.

GREG   He asks for women and the ability to dance too. We try not to give in to him.

SARAH   Mr. Harrison. Would it amaze you to know that seventy percent of quadriplegics get better care in a nursing home where they can be attended to? Seventy percent have a better quality of life. Studies say that they may even live longer? Did you know that? And the burden on the state is significantly less. You receive upwards of thirty thousand in benefits…

GREG   I don't think so.

SARAH   The bed, the equipment. The visits.

GREG   We refused the visits.

SARAH   Yes, but they're still available to you, whether you use them or not. I'm looking at this paper, here. Thirty thousand in benefits but a care home, a home that would give him a better value of life, a better standard of care, twenty-four hour care, would cost the taxpayer about a third of that.

GREG   I don't see how that…

SARAH   I completely understand. What you're saying makes perfect sense. It does. But for families as well. Studies have shown that relieved of the burden of being a care giver makes family members better suited to give care, if you follow what I mean. How old were you when you had Gareth, Mr. Harrison?

GREG   Nineteen.

SARAH   (NODDING) Your wife was seventeen. What I mean is; given all that; what you've achieved… it's fantastic. It really is. But you're a young man. Your wife was a young woman. Sailing, fishing… more. I'm saying that there's lots you might like to achieve. You're still a young man. Gareth might live another ten years. With the right kind of care, he might live the next twenty. The better quality of life he has, the better quality of life you have…

GREG   Look. I've got to get to work. Yeah.

SARAH   I… Of course, I was hoping to have a word with Gareth, Mr. Harrison.

GREG   I've got to get to work.

SARAH   I can let myself out.

GREG   He's sleeping.

SARAH   (BEAT) No, of course. That's no problem. I can come back? Perhaps on your day off?

GREG   I think we're fine.

SARAH   Mr. Harrison. This is going to happen. It's natural to be frightened of change. It's natural, but the taxpayers are not going to keep footing the bill of health care when better can be given at a better rate.

GREG   We're better left alone.

SARAH   I'm not saying you're not. But I do need to make an assessment. A report, you understand? And to do that I need to speak…

GARETH IS PERCHED ON THE END OF THE BED. LOOKING VERY BIRDLIKE. ON HIS ANKLE A HEAVY ROPE IS TIED. HE IS LOOKING AT THE SKY, THE ROPE BOTHERING HIM.

ABOVE HIM THE BUTTERFLY FLUTTERS.

GREG   Thursday.

SARAH   You're off Thursday?

GREG   Thursday.

GARETH   Little shit! Come on. It's not… I don't need to fly. Flying's not it!

SARAH   (RISING TO LEAVE) Thursday it is. Alright then, Mr. Harrison. I'll look forward to seeing you then.

LIGHTS DOWN ON TABLE.

SCENE 4

THE BUTTERFLY REMAINS OUT OF GARETH'S REACH.

GARETH   If you think you can stay up there all day, you're wrong! Completely wrong! Gravity doesn't work like that! Eh, eh? Oh I know that's what you're thinking but that doesn't make it right, does it? No. No knot in the world's going to keep… Come down here, you little shit! Come down! I'm not going to… Da! Da!!! I can't… Come down here! Right now! You understand me. It's childish, that's what it is! You're being childish! I swear! The minute I get this… fucking… Da. DA!!! You think I don't know what you're doing!? I know what you're doing! I know everything about you! Da!!

ENTER GREG.

GREG ENTERS BUT UNLIT GOES TO THE BED AND IGNORING THE DREAMING GARETH TRIES TO WAKE HIM IN HIS BED.

GARETH MEANWHILE IS NOW FRANTIC WITH THE KNOT, TRYING TO FLY BUT TIED TO THE BED WITH IT.

GARETH   It's not walking! It's not! Come back down here! Come back down here now!

GREG   Gareth!

GARETH   Come back down here! Da!?

GREG   Gareth! Wake up!

GARETH   Come back down here, you little shit!

GREG   Gareth!

GREG PULLS AT THE ROPE AS GARETH JUMPS AND HE COMES CRASHING BACK DOWN TO THE BED.

GREG   (CONT.) Wake up!

GARETH AWAKES.

GREG   (CONT.) Wake up.

GARETH   I was dreaming.

GREG   You were talking in your sleep.

GARETH BEGINS TO CRY SOFTLY. GREG LETS HIM.

GREG   (CONT.) I was… A woman is coming to see you today. From Social Services, like. I think that's where she's from anyway. She had a different name for it.

GARETH   What does she want?

GREG   No idea, really.

GARETH   Tell her to fuck off then.

GREG   I spoke with Stan, like.

GARETH   Aye?

GREG   He's not having the best of times, is he? I was thinking you could have a word with him, like.

GARETH   Me?

GREG   Give him some perspective.

GARETH   Open day at the fuckin' zoo?

GREG   I was thinking… you and I… When your mam was alive, we'd go for walks, like. Along the coastline. Just drive out there and go for walks. She liked that. I never saw the point of it myself. I mean, we'd just drive out and walk. Nothing more, nothing less. All weathers. I think she thought it was healthy, or summut. Make us live longer. When you work at a cannery sea's the last thing you want to smell, but out we'd go. The two of us. In the car. Once every couple of days. Mile along the headland and back. I kind of stopped after she… didn't see the point. Now I wonder if that was the right thing to do.

GARETH   What time is she coming?

ENTER SARAH.

SARAH MARCHES OVER AND DRAWS THE CURTAINS, CASTING NEW LIGHT OVER THE BED.

GREG   Ten or so, I think.

GARETH   I'll let him know she's coming.

SARAH   That's better.

GREG   Mrs… Sarah. This is my son. Gareth.

GARETH   I'd get up, but…

SARAH   It's cold in here.

GARETH   You opened the curtains.

GREG   He likes it.

GARETH   By 'he' he means 'him' not me. I hate the cold. Makes my bloody nose itch.

GREG   We bring a heater in in winter.

SARAH   Isn't it winter, now?

GARETH   Not from these parts, then? Got a saying for it, round here; it's not winter till your piss freezes.

SARAH   Perhaps, Greg, perhaps I can speak to Gareth alone.

GREG   I'll put the kettle on, then.

GARETH   You don't mind if I stay, then?

SARAH   You're not Gareth?

GREG   It's…

GARETH   It's a game we play. Nothing else.

EXIT GREG.

GARETH   (CONT.) You see; my body? Its functions? They all work perfectly. Liver, kidneys… other stuff, all of it. Stuff no one has any control over, you don't either. But, unlike you, I can't even clench. So; it's like another person is attached to me. Gareth.

SARAH   And what does that make you?

GARETH   Redundant. What can I do for you, Ms..?

SARAH   Sarah, please.

GARETH   Dad's a simple man, Sarah. I'm not. Existence is enough for him. Man's barely even travelled. Not on land anyway. Sees things in black and white, you understand? For me, they're a little less clear so you'll excuse me if I greet your visit with scepticism.

SARAH   It's funny you should say that. About your father.

GARETH   What?

SARAH   That existence is enough for him. I didn't get that impression. That's not the image I got from him.

GARETH   You got an image from him!?

SARAH   I got the idea that he was; not to be too indelicate, but that he was sacrificing his life, his happiness to look after his son. That he was living here, with you, out of a sense of obligation. A sense of duty. That he was, in essence, ruining his life.

GARETH   (PAUSE) Go fuck yourself.

SARAH   It's… I know, it's hard. It's…

GARETH CLOSES HIS EYES.

GARETH   There is, up there, a stain. It wasn't there in the summer, and it'll be gone again in spring. Right now it's about seven centimetres by ten and in the mild shape of an upended giraffe but by February it will be double that size and look far more like an aggrieved rabbit. (OPENING THEM AGAIN) Dust on that window ledge takes about ten days of gathering before it really pisses me off but I'm mildly irritated by about day three. If, however, anyone touches it before day six I go insane so I don't like to mention it. (OPENING HIS EYES) Today's day nine.

SARAH   That doesn't stop it being true. I've visited… we work with hundreds of patients. All across the country. All of them in this exact situation. All of them locked in this senseless, expensive… routine! The window? The dust? This is what I'm talking about. The same thing day in, day out… Your body, and you'll have to forgive me here, your body is a prison. Your life doesn't have to be one as well. Imagine… Imagine watching the same TV program day in, day out. You'd get bored by it. But that's what you're doing to yourself here. That's what you're inflicting on yourself! The same scene in the same film over and over, and not particularly a good one, either. That's what you've got. But it doesn't have to be like that.

GARETH   I'd like you to go now.

SARAH   This won't take much longer.

GARETH   Now, please.

SARAH   Just a few more minutes. This. The room, the equipment, the funding, the visits; this is the most costly way of living, and it's the least satisfying. For you, for the people around you, the least satisfying! You, your father, your village, your doctors, me, the taxpayer. This is the worst of all scenarios. Change the channel. Change it! Let us do that for you. For half the price of your prison cell here we can put you in a facility that will… allow you to change the channel! Allow you to see new things, new people. Interact! Allow your father to interact! I checked around. At the cannery? You know how much he's earning? You know how many hours they keep him on for? They don't need him. He's a longboat man. He's not trained for a modern cannery! They keep him on because… well, because. They keep him on out of pity; for you, for him. Since your mother…

GARETH   What you know about my mother!?

SARAH   Your mother died. Of a heart attack. She died of a broken heart. Looking after you. Is that what you want for him?

GARETH   My mother didn't die of a heart attack!

SARAH   I'm sorry?

GARETH   My mother. She didn't die of a heart attack.

SARAH   I thought…

GARETH   She hung herself. Right here. This very room.

SARAH   I'm sorry?

GARETH   She hung herself. Right where you're sitting. Well, not right there, about four feet to the left, but with that very chair.

SARAH   The report said…

GARETH   I was sleeping. When she came in, I was sleeping. She was always… light on her feet… I woke up. I guess, the chair, the noise of the chair. She just hung there… twisting. Her hands moved up to reach the… reach the… but she forced them down again. I don't know if she could hear me. She just hung there. Five hours. Still as I am now. My father… Greg, he cut her down.

SARAH   (PAUSE) Why wasn't this in the report?

GARETH   Everyone went to school with everyone round here. The doctor? He's my father's best friend in secondary. We thought if Social Services find out they'd want to take me away. (SARCASTIC) Guess he was wrong about that, though!

SARAH   Is that why you wanted to kill yourself? After your mother died?

GARETH   Wouldn't you?

SARAH   It says in your file you asked for assisted suicide.

GARETH   Files don't tell you everything.

SARAH   You asked your care worker for a bottle of pills.

GARETH   I thought hanging'd be problematic.

SARAH   Just before she left.

GARETH   They thought I'd be better on my own.

SARAH   No. Your father thought you'd be better on your own. He asked that they stop the visits. He said that the visits were the thing causing your depression.

GARETH   This one is.

SARAH   Did you know he cancelled the visits?

GARETH   Even matricide has a statute of limitations, like.

SARAH   (RISING TO GO) I'm going to leave you now.

GARETH   Tidy.

SARAH   I'm going to leave you, and... I'm sorry. About your mother. The records...

GARETH   We just want to be left alone.

SARAH   I'm going to leave you but, I'll be back. At the end of the week. I hope we can become friends.

GARETH   I'd like that! Unfortunately he's already made up his mind.

SARAH   Goodbye, Gareth.

SCENE 5

AT THE TABLE, GREG AND STAN ARE SITTING, DRINKING TEA.

STAN IS MUCH THE SAME AGE AS GARETH BUT ALTHOUGH FIT AND BRIGHT LOOKING HE IS CLEARLY MISSING IN MENTAL FACULTIES WHAT GARETH IS IN PHYSICALITY.

THE PAIR ARE SAD, LOST IN THOUGHT. BAD NEWS HAS JUST BEEN DELIVERED TO STAN.

SARAH ENTERS.

SARAH   Greg?

THE MEN JUMP.

GREG   Sarah. Sorry, I missed you there.

SARAH   I think he wants to sleep.

GREG   We were just going over a few things.

STAN   Hello.

GREG   This is Stan. He works at the... Well, he worked at the cannery with me, like.

STAN   Nice to meet you. I'm Stan.

SARAH   Yes, hello.

STAN   No place for me, now.

SARAH   Might we have a word, Mr. Harrison?

GREG   Stan. Now. You go home, alright? Go straight home. No stopping at the pub. Your mother's expecting you.

STAN   My mum cooks me dinner.

SARAH   That's nice.

STAN   Run along now.

GREG   See ya!

SARAH   It's nice to have met you.

STAN   Bye, Mr. Harrison!

GREG   Run along, now.

EXIT STAN.

GREG   All mice and no men, that boy.

SARAH   He worked with you at the cannery?

GREG   Laid him off this morning, they did. Last in, first out.

SARAH   These are tough times for all of us.

GREG   Cuppa? (SHE WAVES HIM AWAY) Hard for his mother, that's the thing. Got him twenty-four seven now. Least before… Course, she's not his real mother. Lovely woman. One of them brides, you know? Mail order. Thailand. Came across about five year ago. Remember when she came here! Couldn't speak a word of English!

SARAH   That's strange, isn't it? A mail-order bride, out here?

GREG   It's a fishing town, miss. You do the math. Thought she'd go, like! After Henry passed. Got a big settlement and everything. Only been here about three years, thought she'd put herself on a plane and that would be that, but stayed on. For the boy. Didn't think he'd take to Thailand, I suppose.

SARAH   Gareth told me about his mother.

GREG   Oh, aye?

SARAH   About her death?

GREG   Ah, he misses her. What can you say? I miss her, too like. Woman's the life of a house. Gives it meaning. Once that was gone from here, well… men don't do communication that well, do they.

SARAH   About his room?

GREG   I'm not following.

SARAH   About her death, in his room.

GREG   (SHAKING HIS HEAD) No. She died on the stairs. Heart attack. Carrying his lunch up. Put it down, sat down and went, I guess.

SARAH   (SUSPICIOUS) He… he told me about the doctor!? His room?

GREG   (UNDERSTANDING) He's got… he's in that room all day, miss. In his head. He's got what you call an active imagination. Why, what'd he come up with this time?

SARAH   I… This isn't a game, Mr. Harrison.

GREG   No one thinks it is.

SARAH   It's quite clear to me that this is an unhealthy situation. For you and Gareth.

GREG   Whatever he told you…

SARAH   It doesn't matter what he told me. What matters is that we get Gareth the best care. And it's clear that isn't here. He needs to be moved. To a care facility! Where he can get proper attention.

GREG   If that happens..?

SARAH   (MAKING TO LEAVE) It's going to happen. The fiscal year ends and there's no more funding. Either he's in a home by the end of the fiscal year or there's no more funding.

GREG   But… the house…

SARAH   It's the best thing for all of you. Mr. Harrison. My recommendation is you get used to it. Quickly.

EXIT SARAH.

GREG STANDS THERE. SHOCKED.

END OF ACT 1.

ACT 2

ACT 2

SCENE 1

LIGHTS UP ON THE SHIP OF DREAMS.

AT SEA. GARETH IS ONCE MORE DRESSING HIMSELF IN FRONT OF THE MIRROR.

ENTER GREG.

GREG   Captain!

GARETH   Mr. Harrison. Do you have her?

GREG   That we do, Captain!

GARETH   Very well. Bring her to me.

GREG   Captain?

GARETH   Bring her to me Mr. Harrison! I want to see my attacker face to face!

GREG   Is that wise Captain? She was sent here to kill you!

GARETH   All women are, Mr. Harrison. Longevity is not what we're looking for when a gentleman meets a lady. Well, not that kind of longevity anyway. Show her in.

GREG   Yes, Captain.

EXIT GREG.

GARETH CONTINUES TO GET DRESSED. AS HE DOES GREG RE-ENTERS WITH SARAH

GREG   Captain.

GARETH   Ah. So, this is the woman who's been trying to kill me?

SARAH   Without much success.

GARETH   (MOTIONING TO THE BED) Would you?

SARAH   It's a bed. You don't have anything more... upright?

GARETH   The plank?

SARAH   The bed it is then. (SHE FLOPS INTO IT) So, this is the boudoir of the infamous Captain Gareth.

GARETH   Infamy is overrated.

SARAH   You must have had hundreds of women through here.

GARETH   (SMILING) Only in dreams.

SARAH   It can't last you know.

GARETH   Nothing good does.

GREG   I'll go then, shall I?

GARETH   No. Stay.

SARAH   Go.

EXIT GREG.

GARETH   I wanted him to stay.

SARAH   Everything good goes.

GARETH   Who says he's good?

SARAH   Look at you. The great Captain! Stuck here. The whole world out there for him and where is he? Sitting on a boat in the middle of the sea.

GARETH   It's called an ocean.

SARAH   I'm not a sailor.

GARETH   Where would you have me? There's a bounty on my head. Two of the world's deadliest assassins want me dead. Where better to be than in bed… rhyming.

SARAH   A real man would be out there. Living his life. Letting the world get the better of him.

GARETH   Who says I'm a real man! So; Miss…

SARAH   Harrison.

GARETH   Miss… (TROUBLED) Harrison. Tell me about yourself.

SARAH   There's not much to tell. I killed my first man at the age of fourteen, in a bathroom in Istanbul. My second I ran through with a poker. There's not a man who's been able to escape me; until you.

GARETH   When you died…

THERE IS A GREAT COMMOTION OFF, AS IF THE SHIP IS RATTLING, THEY BOTH FALL AROUND AS THE FLOOR BENEATH THEM BECOMES UNSTEADY.

THE LIGHTS FLASH ON AND OFF, THE DREAM CHANGING TO A NIGHTMARE.

SARAH   What's happening?

GARETH   (SCARED) If this is you…

SARAH   (SCARED) It's not, I swear.

GARETH   If this is you..!

SARAH   It's not!

THEY BOTH LOOK OFF.

SARAH   It's him isn't it. He's finally here for you.

GARETH   Go out and check!

SARAH   You want me to go out there?

GARETH   Just stick your head out!

SARAH   He'll kill me.

GARETH   Stay here and I'll kill you!

SARAH   What do you want me to tell him?

GARETH   What do I care? Just get out there and stop him.

SILENTLY SARAH GETS UP AND HEADS OFF-STAGE. AS SHE DOES SO, LIGHTS BLIND THE AUDIENCE AND THE NOISE INCREASES.

SCENE 2

THE HOUSE.

STAN IS STANDING OVER THE BED, SHAKING GARETH.

GARETH   Stan? Stan. You can stop shaking me now.

STAN   You was sleeping.

GARETH   Hello Stan.

STAN   Your dad says you want to talk to me.

GARETH   Give me a minute, Stan, yeah?

STAN   You okay? You was sweating.

GARETH   Give me a moment.

STAN WANDERS AROUND THE ROOM. GARETH COMPOSES HIMSELF, REIGNING IN THE FEAR.

STAN SEES SOMETHING UNDER THE BED.

STAN   Oh, look. (HE BENDS TO PICK IT UP) Gar, Gar? You remember this? We used to play with it in your garden. You remember? Look, Gar?

GARETH   It's a ball.

STAN   It's the ball we used to play. In the garden. When we were children.

GARETH   Stan, can you… I need something to drink.

STAN   Right you are then. I'll put it here, shall I? (HE PUTS IT ON THE BED) You can look at it later.

GARETH   Thank you.

STAN   (MOTIONING TO THE GLASS) This water?

GARETH   Please.

STAN   You want me to hold it for you?

GARETH   Please… closer.

STAN   Right.

IT'S A STRUGGLE BUT HE MANAGES TO DRINK.

GARETH   Thank you.

STAN GIGGLES AS HE SPILLS SOME OVER GARETH.

STAN   You want more?

GARETH   (HURRIEDLY) No. Thank you.

STAN   Fancy that, eh! The ball. After all these years.

GARETH   What do want, Stan?

STAN   Your dad says I should talk to you. Thinks it might cheer you up, he does.

GARETH   He did, did he?

STAN   Cos, I'm good like that. Talking to people.

GARETH   Oh, aye? How's the job at the cannery?

STAN   Don't work there no more.

GARETH   No?

STAN   (ANGERED AT THE TEASING) No! (SOFTER) First in, last out. That's important. People aren't eating fish. (PAUSE) I liked that job. Working with your dad, yeah. I liked that. Store can't take me back either. Closed. Thai mum says she'll try to find me something but...

ENTER SARAH.

SARAH ENTERS CARRYING SHAVING EQUIPMENT AND A LAPTOP BAG.

SARAH   Hello again.

STAN   Hello.

GARETH   Stan's an old friend.

SARAH   We've met.

GARETH   Sarah's a government stooge.

SARAH   We prefer the term 'lackey'. Stan, do you mind? I'd like to talk to Gareth alone.

STAN (CLEARLY UNCOMFORTABLE) No. No. (TO GARETH) I'll leave the ball there for you, shall I?

GARETH   Thank you, Stan.

EXIT STAN.

GARETH   (LOOKING AT THE BOWL) What's that for?

SHE PUTS THE LAPTOP BAG ON THE BED NEXT TO THE BALL AND STRAIGHTENS THE CLOTHING.

SARAH   You need a shave.

GARETH   I need a lot of things. Are we expecting company?

SARAH   Your father thought it would be good for you.

GARETH   He did, did he?

SARAH   You don't mind?

GARETH   You've shaved a lot of men, have you?

SARAH   Don't be such a baby! (SHE STARTS TO PREPARE HIM FOR SHAVING) In answer to your question… don't move… in answer to your question. My father. I used to shave my father.

GARETH   When was this?

SARAH   In England. He got old. Couldn't cope by himself.

GARETH   That was nice of you. To do that.

SARAH   Stop moving! Yes, well, the nurses at the home weren't that good at it. I suppose they had a lot of people to get through every day… (SHE NEEDS TO MOVE HIS HEAD) May I?

GARETH   It won't move itself.

SILENCE.

SARAH   You know, I was reading about conjoined twins. There are two girls in America; conjoined and they live… perfectly normal lives.

GARETH   You're   not   seriously   comparing quadriplegics to twins?

SARAH   My point is; they get along. Their situation is their situation and they get along.

GARETH   This is my home. I was born here. I'll die here. I would have died here a long time ago if they'd let me.

SARAH   This is the world. This is where we are! There's no point being maudlin about it. Your life, as it is, can be better. It will be better. You'll meet new people…

GARETH   Kill me with kindness why don't you.

SHE CUTS HIM PURPOSEFULLY.

GARETH   Ow.

SARAH   I'm sorry. I told you not to move.

GARETH   One square foot of real estate I can feel pain on and you had to find it.

SARAH   Don't be such a baby.

PAUSE. GARETH LOOKS UP AT SARAH AS SHE TENDS TO THE CUT.

GARETH   You married?

SARAH   I'm nearly done. (SHE CONTINUES SHAVING) I have a present for you. In that bag over there.

GARETH   What is it?

SARAH   Greg… your father… he gave me some of your stories to read. The ones you've been writing? I asked if I could read them and he gave me some.

GARETH   It's just writing.

SARAH   You've quite the imagination on you, haven't you? Pirates!

GARETH   What is it; the present?

SARAH   It's a laptop.

SHE HESITATES, SEEING SHE NEEDS TO STRAIGHTEN HIS HEAD. THEN SHE DOES SO, GENTLY.

GARETH   Fuck am I going to do with porn?

SARAH   A computer is so much more practical than those papers. I doubt that anyone can read your handwriting. If you're going to have a creative mind, you might as well put it to use.

GARETH   I'm supposed to use it how, like?

SARAH   It's a special one. With a fitted mouth piece. It's got a tongue depressor. Voice software. You can get quite fast. I'll set it up once we're done here.

GARETH   Do you have any idea what this is like?

SARAH   Of course I do.

GARETH   Being out there in the world? Living? You know what this is like?

SARAH   You have an imagination. Use it. (PAUSE) It was cruel. What you said before.

GARETH   What?

SARAH   About your mother. If you want to use your imagination, use it. But that was cruel.

GARETH   You're the one trying to take me from my home.

SARAH   I'm trying to show you... How many countries have you been to? Hmm? Spain, France... I took a trip to Milan once for a conference but that's it for me. That's all there was. The rest... But you, you went everywhere! Asia, Europe...

GARETH   And look where it brought me! If I had never left...

SARAH   We don't do self-pity in my house

GARETH   In my house it's pretty much all we have. You don't think I'm entitled?

SARAH   No one is entitled to anything. Your father says you've been writing them since your mum died: the stories. I can edit them for you if you like.

DONE, SHE IS ABOUT TO CLEAN UP. SHE STOPS. SMELLING SOMETHING.

GARETH   He needs a change, I suspect.

SARAH   Your conjoined twin.

GARETH   My better half.

SARAH   Save the melodrama for the page. Use that imagination for something other than self-pity.

PAUSE.

GARETH   And after I write them?

SARAH   We publish them. Local newspaper… internet… They'd make a great human interest piece.

GARETH   What you get out of this? The laptop? The visits?

SARAH   You don't think I care?

GARETH   I think you get paid no matter what.

SARAH   It's so sad, isn't it? To see someone's given up.

GARETH   Given up?

SARAH   Given up! Life's tough. For all of us. We scratch, we fight, we bleed out an existence, a life. What I don't understand… I don't understand shopkeepers who look like they don't want to be there. I don't understand people who have to be somewhere, working, and then spend all their time complaining about it. I don't understand how they can do that?! They have to be there! Or at least, they have to be there if they want to get paid for it so you might as well make the best out of it! You rely on the kindness of strangers. You rely on your father to look after you, the council to pay him to do it, but all you can be is rude to people! Sullen! I don't understand how you can treat people the way you treat people when the only thing you've got going for you are the people around you. The shopkeeper? He can leave his job. You're stuck here. Make the most of it! Now, let's clean you up and we'll take a look at the software, alright? (GARETH WATCHES HER) If it's good… who knows? Put something on the page! Interact.

GARETH   You really think your life is fucking important, don't you!

SARAH   I think; in the past couple of weeks, since I've been here, your life has improved. I think you're happier than you've been in years right now and these dreams? The ones you want to want to live in? I bet they're happier too. Write something.

GARETH WATCHES AS SHE LEAVES.

END OF ACT 2.

HAPPINESS

ACT 3

ACT 3

SCENE 1

AT THE TABLE.

GREG IS TALKING WITH ANGEL.

ANGEL   He is good boy, you know? He comes home on time. He cleans his room, washes dishes…

GREG   'Cept he isn't a boy, is he.

ANGEL   No. I try, you know? But it is very hard. I'm sorry, I should not.

GREG   Who else? When they were little, they'd play out there, on the hill. Uphill football. Wasn't til about seven or eight that Stan… There weren't the tests then, you know. We knew he was slow but it weren't until about seven it became clear if you follow. He just stopped growing. Inside. My wife… She didn't like him hanging around Didn't like him in the house. Guess she thought it was catching or something. Gareth was; well, he was always bright. Don't know where he got it, myself. His mother was good. Keen, you know, but not with schooling. Gareth though… By eight the gulf between them… Still, they kept on. Ball every night. Uphill. One at top, one at bottom til they scored then they'd switch over. Lots of the boys played. I didn't mind it. Common ground.

Drifted apart a bit, by secondary, you know. Did their best with him; Stan. Did their bit, like, but it's not like it is nowadays. No special needs classes. Gareth got on in school and Stan didn't, but he was still round here. Every few weeks.

Sorry, I'm going on.

ANGEL   Who else?

GREG   (GETTING UP SUDDENLY) Don't you miss them? Your family?

ANGEL   My hometown. It is much like this. Without weather. Do I miss them? Of course I miss them. They are my family, you know? I send them money.

GREG   Don't you miss the weather?

ANGEL   Of course I miss the weather! I miss the food.

GREG   You should take him. Take the boy! Life's not going to be that much different out there for him. Not like there's anything for him to do here, is there.

ANGEL   You don't know. When I came here... There are lights all across my hometown. Lots of lights. Mountains too. If you are looking at night there is no difference between here and my hometown. Mountains and sea. Mountains and sea. But the lights. Here there are pockets. One, two, three lights. Back home it's more like; one light. One light made up of lots, you know? You can't forget that, you know? And the smell... totally different here. Everything. My sisters? I'm the adventurous one, you know that? I have an older sister. She should be married first, but I'm the adventurous one! I'm the wild one so I get married first. Get out. My sister, she much more shy. She would never be able to live here, you know? She would die. You can't put someone in a bottle all their lives and then just take them out, you know? You can't do that!

GREG   No.

ANGEL   What you gonna do about your son?

GREG   Don't know.

ANGEL   Maybe home is better for him.

GREG   It's not.

ANGEL   Maybe it is.

GREG   I keep remembering… We had this dog, when I was a boy. My father. He was a great dog. Peaceful. Gentle. Playful he was. But he was a farm dog, you know what I mean? Proper farm dog. Job was to guard things, scare people, not to go up to them. So, we broke him. Had to, like. It was that or put him down. Every day my father would give him a treat, hold out his hand with a treat or pet him, something he liked, and then he'd beat him. Treat, beat him. Treat, beat him. Meanest dog you've ever seen. Gareth was like that. When he came back. We had to break him. Sixteen and he hitchhiked to London. All the way, on his own. Didn't tell us nothing about it. By eighteen he'd been to more places than I'll ever go. Ever want to go! So when he came back here. When they brought him back from Germany. We had to break him, see? He was a wanderer. What they call a free spirit. But there's nothing free about him now. He stayed like that he'd have gone insane. Was going insane. So we had to break him. Shut him in. Lock him off. Worries me that, sometimes. Line between people and dogs.

ANGEL   It's the drinking. I try not to give him money. I try to keep… I don't allow it in the house but people are nice, you know? They buy him drinks. At the pub! It's not good. They think they are being kind, but they're not. When he is sober, it's not so bad, you know? But the drink… It's not good. He's a big boy!

GREG   You are good to stay with him. Henry'd

appreciate that.

ANGEL   (LAUGHING) Henry don't care. He is like your dog, you know? Mean.

GREG   Yeah, I guess he was, like.

ANGEL   Death was best thing about him. You know?

GREG   Why'd you stay?

ANGEL   Who else?

LIGHTS UP ON SHIP OF DREAMS AND HOUSE.

DREAM TIME.

THE BEDROOM IS NOW THE DECK OF A SHIP. THE BED THE WHEEL HOUSE. GARETH SITS ON THE END OF THE BED, LOOKING OUT ACROSS THE OCEAN. STAN IS BEHIND HIM, STEERING THE SHIP.

ALTHOUGH BOTH PEACEFUL, BOTH OF GARETH' LEGS ARE NOW TIED TO THE BED.

COMPLETELY RELAXED, HE WATCHES AS THE BUTTERFLY FLUTTERS IN FRONT OF HIM.

GARETH   Keep course Mr. Evans.

STAN   What's our course, Captain?

GARETH   The second star you see, Mr. Evans.

STAN   Aye, aye Captain!

BACK AT THE TABLE.

ANGEL   Why you never been to other countries? You sail everywhere, you know?

GREG   Does Iceland count?

ANGEL   Iceland? That don't sound like a real country.

STAN   Where we going, Captain?

GREG   No fish on land. Fishermen stay at sea. Only port you use is your home dock.

STAN   Captain?

GARETH   I can't remember. I... There used to be... She was extraordinary. To me, at least. This... frailty. Completely undone, like pieces of a person held together by strength alone. Vulnerable but... this amazing strength. To just hold it all together. I told her; "I own one part of you. That's all. The time you give me. Nothing more." Only in German. Why can't I speak German anymore? She was... It was as if she'd thrown every kind of hurt she could at herself and then... rebuilt it. I remember thinking, when I met her: eventually you'll kill yourself. You'll either find a way to kill yourself or you'll kill the part of you that's trying to.

STAN   Is she on the charts?

ANGEL   Would you go somewhere? If you could?

GARETH   I couldn't even tell you what she looked like now.

GREG   Where would you go? Home?

ANGEL   Home. If I could, you know? Dreams are important.

GREG   Dreams are pointless.

STAN   We're going to run aground in a minute.

GARETH   (LOOKING AT THE ROPES) It doesn't

matter.

THEY RUN AGROUND.

BLACKOUT.

SCENE 2

THE HOUSE.

NIGHT. GARETH IS IN BED. THE REST OF THE HOUSE IS PITCHED IN BLACK.

STAN IS SITTING ON THE END OF THE BED, A CAN OF BEER IN HIS HAND AND THE REMNANTS OF A SIX PACK IN THE OTHER. HE IS OBVIOUSLY DRUNK.

GARETH   Stan?

STAN   Fuckster.

GARETH   Stan, what time is it.

STAN   S'alright for you. You got it lucky. That's what you got. That's what you got.

GARETH   Stan, does my Dad know you're here?

STAN   (CHANGING DEMEANOUR) Gar, Gar. Hey. Hey. Shhh. I brought... I brought you a drink. You want a drink?

GARETH   What do you want Stan.

STAN   No, look, I brought you a drink!

GARETH   (LOUD) Dad!

STAN   (ANGRILY COVERING GARETH'S MOUTH) Shh. No. No! I brought you a drink. You remember? I used to… (HE RELEASES HIM) I found that ball for you. Couple of weeks back? You still got that ball? You still got it, hmm?

GARETH   Stan… it's… it's late, yeah, maybe we can talk about this in the morning, like.

STAN   Thought we could have a game of catch.

GARETH   Sure. Go long!

STAN   I ain't got nothing to do! Nothing. Thai mum. She's gonna leave me, you know? You know? You know! That's all she ever says. You know! It's just… it's… stupid, stupid, stupid.

GARETH   Stop it, man. She's not going anywhere.

STAN   What do you know!? You don't know nothing you don't!

GARETH   She's stayed this long, hasn't she?

STAN Yeah, but it's the drink. The drink! The drink! Innit. She don't like the drink! Don't trust it, you know, but I got to… I liked working with your Dad, you know? He was good to me.

GARETH   Sure, munn.

STAN   (MENACING AGAIN) Look, I got you a drink.

GARETH   I'm fine.

STAN   (OPENING A CAN MENACINGLY) No, look. It's like the water!

GARETH   (SCARED) No, Stan.

STAN   It's like the water. Here. Here!

HE POURS SOME INTO GARETH'S MOUTH.

GARETH   (SPLUTTERING) Stop it!

STAN   (MALICIOUSLY POURING) No, look.
Look. I got you a drink. I got you a drink!

LIGHTS COME ON.

ENTER GREG.

STAN STOPS, GARETH GAGS.

STAN   I got him a drink.

GREG   (QUIETLY) Go downstairs.

STAN SHEEPISHLY EXITS AFRAID OF THE HIT
THAT NEVER COMES.

GREG   You alright?

GARETH   Would have preferred whisky.

GREG   I'll be back to clean you in a minute.

GARETH   Alright.

GREG   I'd better…

GARETH   Yeah.

EXIT GREG.

SCENE 3

AT THE TABLE.

STAN IS WAITING. ANXIOUS. CLOSE TO GIGGLING. HE HAS A CAN IN HIS HAND.

ENTER GREG.

GREG   What you doing in my house, Stan?

STAN   Greg…

GREG   What are you doing in my house?

STAN SCARED DRINKS FROM THE CAN. GREG REACHES OUT.

GREG   (CONT.) I need you to give me that. I can't talk to you when you're like this. Give it to me!

STAN DOES KEEPING THE CAN HE'S HOLDING.

GREG SETS THE CANS DOWN IN THE KITCHEN THEN HOLDS OUT HIS HAND AGAIN.

GREG   (CONT.) That one and all.

GARETH TAKES ONE LAST GUILTY GLUG THEN HANDS IT OVER.

GREG   (CONT.) That's better. Alright. Stan. You can't just come in here whenever you want.

STAN   Why not?

GREG   You know why not. Gareth…

STAN   We're mates.

GREG   You're not. You're not, Stan. You're not boys anymore. You can't be up there like this. You shouldn't be anywhere like this. Listen, Stan… sit. Would you, sit? I'm not going to do anything to you. Please? (STAN SITS) That's better. Listen, you and I; we're friends, right? Your mother and me…

STAN   She's not my mum.

GREG   Alright.

STAN   She's Thai mum.

GREG   Your mum and me, we're friends, like. All of us. But Gareth… He can't play with you like he used to. You know that.

STAN   I know that.

GREG   You know that. Do you… Christ, I'm bad at this… Do you miss your Dad, is that it? Is it Henry? You're a big lad now, Stan. You can't be carrying on like this. Angel? When you're like this? She's scared of you. You could hurt someone! I know that's not what you want to do. But you could hurt someone! You could hurt Gareth. You were hurting him! Do you understand that? Henry was… Henry. Doesn't have to be like that. Your… mum, Angel, she's… she's a good woman. A really good woman.

STAN   She's gonna go.

GREG   Why do you say that, like?

STAN   She's gonna go. She's not from round here. She's a chinky fuck.

GREG   Don't talk like that.

STAN   She's gonna go. She's like the rice food. You know the rice food? She's like that. That's what she is, and she's gonna go. Back to that.

GREG   Maybe… maybe she could take you with her? Ever thought about that, like?

STAN   I'm not rice food.

GREG   No. No, me neither, I guess. You remember

Dai, right? Scot's boy?

STAN   He's locked up.

GREG   Yes, yes he is. They're gonna do that to you, too. Keep on like this; they're gonna have to!

STAN   Like Gareth.

GREG   I suppose so. Yes.

STAN   He can't leave.

GREG   Not his fault.

STAN   He's stuck here an' all.

GREG   It's not the same thing. Gareth… Gareth didn't do anything wrong. You know? He had an accident. It happens. But you, you got control over this. When… if they lock you up, it'll be because they have to. Not because of an accident.

STAN   We used to play. Gareth and me. We used to play out there on the hill. Down by the fishing. We used to steal beer out the back of the pub. When we were little, like. They put them crates out back before it opens and we just take 'em. Still do, you know, when I have to.

GREG   Stan…

STAN   And she's not my mum. She's not and it's good. Good. She was good to my dad.

GREG   Stan.

STAN   Good for him, you know? You know? 'You know?' (LAUGHS)

GREG   Stanley!

STAN   But she's gonna go. She is. She's gonna go.

And they'll lock me away. Like... Like David. Like you lock Gareth away.

GREG   Listen!

STAN   Why don't we sail?

GREG   What?

STAN   Sail. In your boat. Just me and you! Two buds, out on the water. You'd like that.

GREG   I don't...

STAN   You'd like that! You'd like it and I'd like it... just sailing. You, me...

GREG   I think you'd better leave.

STAN   You don't want him here!

GREG   Who?

STAN   Gareth.

GREG   Don't say that!

STAN   You don't. You're like Thai mum. She never looks at me... you never look at me like that.

GREG   You're drunk, man.

STAN   We can take Gareth, if you want? The three of us...

GREG   (STANDING) Go home, Stan. We'll say no more about it, alright.

STAN   (MOVING TO LEAVE) Alright.

STAN STOPS AT THE DOOR.

STAN   (CONT.) Can I have my beer.

GREG   (ANGRY FOR THE FIRST TIME) Go

home, Stanley. Your mother'll be worried.

EXIT STAN.

FADE TO BLACK.

END OF ACT 3.

ACT 4

ACT 4

SCENE 1

LIGHTS UP ON THE TABLE.

ANGEL AND GREG ARE BEING QUESTIONED
BY A POLICEMAN.

POLICE   (TO GREG) And it was your boat, then?

GREG   Yes.

POLICE   You loaned it to him?

GREG   I didn't. No. No. He, umm… was talking
about it.

POLICE   When was this?

GREG   Last night, like.

POLICE   Here.

GREG   He… he was drunk. He came here. I… I
don't know, I should have known.

POLICE   Known? Known what?

GREG   Should have known, that's all.

POLICE   I just thought… what with you and the
dyings…

ANGEL   What?

GREG   Leave it alone, man.

PAUSE.

ANGEL   Is there any chance…

PAUSE.

GREG   She's talking about the body.

POLICE   It'll wash up eventually. Tides and everything. Can't say where. You know how it is.

GREG   No.

POLICE   So he came here in the middle of the night? What you talk about?

GREG   My boat. We talked about my boat.

POLICE   How many boats do you have?

GREG   Just one.

POLICE   Yeah? What you got?

GREG   You saw it didn't you.

POLICE   Coast guard sees to that. I'm just here for the statement.

GREG   Highlander four six five.

POLICE   Oh, aye? My dad used to have a highlander. Yamaha?

GREG   Tohatsu.

POLICE   Really? Get better torque with a Yamaha. Always had problems with the electrics, my Dad?

GREG   Run them off a separate battery.

POLICE   That right? So he talked about the boat?

GREG   Aye.

POLICE   Didn't say where he was going or something?

ANGEL   That's enough, you know? He could barely

sail! He was… he was a child.

POLICE PAUSES.

POLICE   We'll have to interview your son.

GREG   You think he pushed him off, do you?

POLICE   It's procedure.

ANGEL   He doesn't know anything.

POLICE   It's just procedure, miss. And you were…
his stepmother?

ANGEL/GREG Yes.

POLICE   And you're a citizen? I mean; you have
papers? It's just routine.

ANGEL   I'm a British citizen!

POLICE   Not Welsh?

GREG   That's enough, yeah.

POLICE GETS UP TO LEAVE.

POLICE   We recover the body we'll let you know, but
given the tides and time, along with the water temperature,
I think there's very little… well. (TO GREG) You'll
explain, yeah?

GREG   Thank you. (SEEING HIM OUT) Um,
the boat.

POLICE   Coasts guards got to hold it until they're
done with it but you can pick it up after that. You'll have
to talk to them about charges.

GREG   Good night.

POLICE GOES TO LEAVE AND PAUSES.

POLICE   No rope marks this time. Around the neck, like. Must be getting better at it.

GREG   Good night.

EXIT POLICE.

GREG TURNS AND IS SURPRISED TO SEE ANGEL QUIETLY CRYING.

GREG   (UNCOMFORTABLE) Least they left Gareth alone, eh? (PAUSE) It's… he'd have gone quickly. The cold this year. Would have been over in a minute. I…. I'm sorry.

ANGEL   (ANGRY) You let him go! You just let him go! You knew how he was and you just let him go!

GREG   I…

ANGEL   Don't. You know? Don't. He was just a boy!

SILENCE.

ANGEL   (CONT.) I've got to go.

GREG   Please.

ANGEL   I've got to go. (SHE MOVES TO LEAVE AND PAUSES) Just… I need to not see you, you know? I need… At the funeral… I need you not to come, you know?

GREG   I understand.

ANGEL   Goodbye.

SCENE 2

SARAH IS STANDING NEXT TO THE BED. GARETH IS WATCHING AS THE BUTTERFLY FLUTTERS ALONG THE END OF THE BED.

SARAH You must have been in love though. To have said that?

GARETH Don't remember.

SARAH And here's me thinking you were only dead from the neck down.

GARETH I think… people fall in love like this; they get tired, they get scared, the perfect person hasn't come along yet. The supermodel with the mothering complex hasn't knocked on the door. So they take the first person who's interested in them and they ask themselves… Can I put up with this? The fat, the temper, the hair she leaves in the shower; is this better than being alone? Too right it is! And why? Because the idea of being alone is hard-wired into us as a 'bad' thing. I used to like fucking. I used to like being with people. I never thought the two had to be mutually inclusive.

SARAH I don't believe that.

GARETH I rest my case.

SARAH So; shall we open it.

GARETH Now?

SARAH Don't be such a coward.

GARETH Says the one who can walk away.

SHE COMES OVER TO THE BED AND PICKS UP AN ENVELOPE SHE LEFT THERE. SHE OPENS IT

AND UNFOLDS A LETTER, LEAVING IT IN HIS EYE-LINE.

HE READS.

AS HE DOES SO SARAH OPENS THE WINDOW AND AND THE BUTTERFLY FLIES GRATEFULLY OUT.

SARAH   And?

GARETH   "An extraordinary feat." They're publishing it next month.

SARAH   That's fantastic! That's... I'm so pleased for you!

GARETH   They probably liked the edit.

SARAH   It's you they liked!

GARETH   Yeah. Thank you.

SARAH PICKS UP THE LETTER AND READS IT.

SARAH   They want more! You see!? You see what you can do if you put your mind to it? This is the beginning for you. The start! Your life... it can be so much, much more...

GARETH   Or I could become a famous writer and stay where I am.

SARAH   Don't start.

GARETH   Why not?

SARAH   Why are you so resistant to this? We've known each other; what? A couple of weeks, and look what we've achieved!? Look what you've achieved! What you can do?

GARETH   I think that's my point.

SARAH   But it can be so much more. So much, much more than this... your friend...

GARETH   He wasn't my friend.

SARAH   Okay. You're right. Look. There's... this is a good day; yes? A good day?

GARETH   A good day.

SARAH   So let's put one good day next to another and we'll see where it takes us, okay?

GARETH   Okay.

SARAH   I'm gonna talk to your father, okay?

GARETH   Sarah?

SARAH   Yes?

GARETH   The magazine...

SARAH   (MISUNDERSTANDING) Oh, sorry. I'll put it...

GARETH   No, the story. It's because: it's good, right? That's why they want to publish it. Not because...

SARAH   Does it really matter? It's a good story.

GARETH   Yeah, okay.

SHE KISSES HIM ON THE CHEEK.

SARAH   Alright. I'm going to talk to your father.

EXIT SARAH.

SCENE 3

AT THE TABLE GREG IS DRINKING HEAVILY.

SARAH   I think he wants to sleep.

GREG   They liked the story?

SARAH   I told you they would.

GREG   You did, right enough.

SARAH   There's a whole world out there for him. A whole world! I know you think you're doing what you can but I can promise you… I can tell you; it's not what he needs!

GREG   So you say.

SARAH   But you don't believe me.

GREG   I think… I think, being honest; I think this is no life for anyone. We're people. Body up. We get the hands we get and we don't get a say in that. You say we're supposed to do our best with that. You say we're supposed to live better; want better? I agree with you! But we're a family. And family means sacrifice. It's what it means!

SARAH   He can live such a rich life. Such a rich life! These stories…

GREG   Hang on a minute! He's got… my son always had a great imagination. Always. He used to write like crazy, back in the day. He used to write it all down. Sent off everything. All of it. And nothing! You think it's any different now that he's typing with his teeth? Pirates? Pirates? You think that's going to get him anywhere? You know that. I know that. Eventually he's going to work it out and what's that going to do to him then? What's that going to say?

SARAH   It's not your fault. That man…

GREG   Of course it is. Don't be daft. Of course it is! He asked for my help. Stood… right there, where you are… and he asked for my help. His very own words. And I threw him out. Which… You know your problem? You know… You want to throw open the doors and show us the world. Show us what we're missing. What you don't realise is that for most of us, for all of us in here, we were born out there! We were born in the world you want to show us and we've spent most of our lives building the very doors you want to fling open. Don't expect us to say thank you for it! Of course it's my fault! He took my boat and threw himself off the side. It's my fault and there's nothing you or I or anyone can do about it!

SARAH   (REPLACING HIS WHISKY GLASS WITH A MUG OF TEA) This is going to happen, Mr. Harrison. It's going to happen. And… well, I'm sorry if your life is going to seem little without it. I'm sorry about that. You'll have a chance at a better life without him. That's a fact. What you choose to do with it… that's up to you. But it's going to happen. Like it or not. My suggestion is; like it.

EXIT SARAH.

ENTER ANGEL.

ANGEL   She means well, you know?

GREG JUMPS, TRIES TO HIDE THE BOTTLE.

GREG   How long you been there?

ANGEL   She means well.

GREG   Aye, I suppose she does.

ANGEL   I'm sorry about the other day.

GREG   No, no… sit down. Sit down. You look, exhausted.

ANGEL   (PUTTING BOWL ON THE TABLE) I made you this. As a peace.

GREG   No, you didn't have to do that, love… What is it?

ANGEL   It's stew. From my country.

GREG LOOKS AT IT, UNSURE.

GREG   It looks great.

ANGEL   Here. Sit. Sit. (SHE GIVES HIM A SPOON.) Try it!

GREG   Does it not have to be heated or something?

ANGEL   Better cold.

GREG   Oh, joy.

ANGEL   Try it.

GREG TRIES BUT DOESN'T LIKE IT.

ANGEL   (CONT.) I like what you said at the funeral. All the people that came. That was good of them, you know. You too. After what I said. I didn't think you'd come.

GREG   He was well liked.

ANGEL   No, he wasn't. I think he scared most people.

GREG   There's much worse than him.

ANGEL   I meant; scared them. You know? He was

just a boy.

GREG   (DRIBBLING) Mmm, hmm.

ANGEL   You like it?

GREG   Aye, it's great.

ANGEL   You don't have to eat it.

GREG   I'm just full, is all.

ANGEL   Henry was scared of him. Can you believe that? He was. He thought you all looked at him less, you know? Because of him.

GREG   We looked at Henry less for a lot of things.

ANGEL   They turned out for his funeral as well.

GREG   There was nothing on telly.

SILENCE.

ANGEL   So, I'm going back, you know? Packed my bags and everything. An agent will sell the house. The rest can go to charity.

GREG   When are you going?

ANGEL   Tomorrow. Well, tomorrow to Glasgow, then London. I fly out Thursday.

GREG   Will you like it there?

ANGEL   It's home! I won't miss the cold, you know? Or the weather. I won't miss that. (BEAT) You'd like it there! It's very green. Like here. Lots of fields, like here, and the water… well, it's different. Lots of boats, you know? Not the seas you have here. But you'd like it!

GREG   Would I have to eat the food?

ANGEL   She means well.

GREG   Aye.

ANGEL   Maybe if I'd let other people look after
Stan...

GREG   He was family. Well, you treated him like he
was, anyway.

ANGEL   Not that it made much difference.

GREG   You gave him his good years. (PAUSE) He
said something about you, you know. That night. About
me, really. He said... When Henry was around...

ANGEL   You're a good man.

GREG   Am I? Am I? When his mother died... Did
you ever regret, staying with him? Staying here? If you
could take it back? Do you miss him?

ANGEL   You could come with me.

GREG   Where?

ANGEL   If they put him in a home. You'd be... you
might like it.

GREG   Right.

ANGEL   If you wanted to.

GREG   We never got on. Gareth and me. Not when
he was little... I just, I don't know. I wanted kids. I really
did. But we were young. We didn't know what we were
doing, I guess and... somehow I just couldn't connect with
him. I don't think we played more than a couple of hours a
year. I... when he headed off... when he headed off, I was
glad, you know? We were still young. Don't know why we
didn't have another one, really. And... when he came back,

it wasn't so bad. You know? He was… he needed and that's all there was too it. She spent most time with him if I'm being honest. Anyway, it weren't that bad. We got on, like. But without her…

ANGEL   He's lucky to have you.

GREG   I couldn't let him do it. You know? I mean, I got them. The pills and everything. Wasn't that hard. And I thought. Fair enough. It's his life. His way. Who am I to stand in his way on that. I know… if I were in the same position… but… I was…

ANGEL   You were scared that it might be you that wanted him dead.

GREG   Yeah.

ANGEL   You didn't.

GREG   You weren't here, love.

ANGEL   He's lucky to have you.

ANGEL STANDS TO LEAVE.

ANGEL   (CONT.) Anyway. I didn't want to leave it like… last time. You know? You were always good to us. Henry. Stan…

GREG   You'll write?

SHE LEANS IN AND KISSES HIM.

EXIT ANGEL.

SCENE 4

GREG GOES TO THE DOOR AND STANDS LOOKING OUT AT THE COLD NIGHT.

HE WAITS FOR A SECOND AND THEN CALLS OUT.

GREG   Come in, if you're coming.

HE TURNS BACK INTO THE KITCHEN AND BUSIES HIMSELF MAKING ANOTHER CUP OF TEA.

HE'S JUST SET IT DOWN WHEN POLICE ENTERS. CLOSING THE DOOR BEHIND HIM.

GREG   (CONT., WITHOUT TURNING) There's tea on the stove and cans in the fridge. Make of it what you will.

POLICE SITS, WARMS HIS HANDS ON THE CUP, AND THEN TOPS IT UP WITH WHISKY.

POLICE   Shacking up with the widow then, is it? God, it's brass monkeys out there.

GREG   What you doing outside my house, munn?

POLICE   (LOOKING AROUND) How much is this place worth? Couple of hundred? Land like this, top of the hill. Got to be worth a pretty penny!

GREG   You been at the evidence locker again.

GREG MIMICS POLICE, TOPPING UP HIS TEA WITH WHISKEY.

POLICE   Between your house and her's… couple of hundred easy, like.

GREG   You got me all wrong.

POLICE   Do I? Maybe I do. You're a fucking paragon, you know that? Round here? Won't have a bad word said about you! Been working in policing for the last ten years and no one has a bad word about you. No one has nothing bad to say about anything.

GREG   You got me all wrong.

POLICE   I know there's a man upstairs can't move but his head. Know you've been carrying on with the widow twanky. Know her son died off your boat a couple of nights back. That I know. Man who can only move his head might need looking after is what I was thinking.

PAUSE.

GREG   I've known people like you my whole life. Liabilities. Come up every now and again on ship and you have to shake them loose, barnacles we call them.

POLICE   That right?

GREG   People like you; you're not interested in the world around you. Not interested in what's actually going on. Mind like yours needs something bigger than reality. Messier. Can't have you on board a ship. Create a problem just so you can solve it.

POLICE   I saw what I saw.

GREG   There's two hundred Nembutal in the cupboard back there. All prescription. Got them myself. Wasn't hard. You think anyone would even bother to check?

POLICE   I'd check.

GREG   You had your choice last time. Live with it. Let me tell you this; leave it or don't leave it. Sit outside my house or join me in here whenever you want. Spread all the rumours you want about me; but I buried my wife with these hands. I broke the necks of a thousand fish with these hands. I've gutted and peeled and… canned with these two hands. If I was going to do something to someone it'd be open and honest, not skulking around in the shadows with a badge.

PAUSE.

POLICE   (RISING TO LEAVE) Better put something over those onions out there. Frost'll get them if you don't.

GREG   Stew will get them if I do. It's all the same thing.

POLICE   I'll let myself out then.

GREG   I was about done, you know that? Gutted, that's what I was. Gutted on ice.

POLICE   I saw what I saw. Chinky fuck like that and you're welcome… I saw what I saw. Boy was in the way just like she was. (TURNING BACK TO GREG) I get the woman. That I get. I get the insiders. I get… You know what pisses me off, what really gets to me? (HE WAITS FOR AN ANSWER THAT DOESN'T COME) Ten years I've been at this. Ten years! You got dealt a rough hand. A rough hand, and I get that, I get it. But her… Ten years I been at this. What do you call that, then?

GREG   Penance.

POLICE   I saw what I saw. I see anything else, no doctor in the world gonna help you.

EXIT POLICE.

SCENE 5

LIGHTS UP ON THE SHIP OF DREAMS AND HOUSE.

GREG DOESN'T LEAVE. HE RETURNS TO THE TABLE, THE BOTTLE, AND THE STEW.

DREAM TIME.

GARETH IS DANCING WITH SARAH. STAN IS PLAYING ON THE FLOOR.

SONG – 'I COULD HAVE DANCED ALL NIGHT'.

GARETH   And still come back for more... (HE HUMS MORE)

STAN   Come play with me!

GARETH   I'm busy! (TO SARAH) You look beautiful in moonlight, my dear!

STAN   Come play with me!

GARETH   We're too old to play with things. I'm leaving soon anyway.

STAN   Where you going?

GARETH   I don't know. The only thing I know is I'm not staying here. France. Germany... I'm going to just get on a boat and sail. The world's a big place. Where's the First Mate?

GREG   Leave me out of this.

GARETH   There is this girl. In Greece. You won't believe this… we'll make love on a beach. Swim naked in black water… It'll be magical. She has this tattoo… I don't remember what of, but she has this tattoo, right here. A flower or something, and you can see it, just below the water line. Bobbing in the blackness. I've never forgotten her.

STAN   You'll make new friends.

GARETH   We'll still be mates.

STAN   We won't. You'll go off and see the world and it won't be the same when you come back.

GARETH   Who said I'm coming back?

STAN   I won't like you anyway. Not like that. You'll yell. Like my Dad.

GARETH   Don't be stupid. (SHOUTING OFF) First Mate?!

GREG   I'm busy!

SARAH   You want me to stop.

GARETH   I want you to spin me round the moon! But yes, for a minute. First Mate?!

STAN   He's leaving too.

GARETH   Don't be ridiculous!

STAN   He's leaving. You know he is. He's going to sail off. Just like you.

GARETH   Don't be stupid.

STAN   You're stupid.

GARETH   (TO SARAH) Get off me! (OUT) First

Mate!

GREG STORMS UP FROM THE TABLE. HE MOVES QUICKLY AND ANGRILY ACROSS THE STAGE.

GARETH   Ah…

GREG GRABS HIM BY THE THROAT AND THROWS HIM BACKWARD ON TO THE BED.

GARETH   What..!

GREG   Stay down!

GARETH   What are you doing?

GREG   Move and I'll cut it off! Understand me?

HE TAKES THE ROPES FROM THE END OF THE BED AND TIES THEM TO HIS ANKLES.

GARETH   This is insubordination of the highest order! I'll have you strung up from the yard arm!

GREG   (BELLOWING) Shut up!

STAN COMES OVER.

STAN   What are we doing?

GREG   Tie his arms!

HE FINISHES THE OTHER FOOT. SARAH BRINGS ROPES ON FROM THE EDGE OF THE STAGE.

GARETH   Stop it! Stop it! I don't want to do this.

GREG   You think there's anything for you? For people like you? You think there's any chance of escape? You know how long I've been here!? You know how long!? I didn't escape. Your grandfather; he didn't escape! There's only one escape for people like you and me (POINTING AT STAN) and that's his way out. That's what we've got, in bed or out of it. That's all we're ever going to get. You want that escape?

GARETH   No, Dad. Please.

THE ROPES ARE CAST OVER BEAMS AND TIED AROUND HIS WRISTS.

GREG   All that time out there! You think you fooled anyone with that? You think we didn't all know? You're a little boy! No more, no less. And this is where you'll always belong. This is where you'll always be, always was meant to be!

GARETH   I can't feel my feet.

GREG   Did you like it out there? Is that where you want to be?

TOGETHER THEY HAUL HIM UP SO THAT HE IS ELEVATED ABOVE THE BED, STRETCHED FROM HIS LIMBS LIKE A SAIL ABOVE THE BOAT.

GARETH   Please. Don't do this. Don't. Please. Please!

GREG   Walk! Come on! Just get up and walk, if that's what you want!

GARETH   I can't!

GREG   I can't hear you?

GARETH   Please.

GREG   Go if you want to go!

GARETH   I don't want to go?!

GREG   Is that what you like?

GARETH   I'm scared!

GREG   Is that what you want!

GARETH   I want to stay.

GREG   It's too late for that. It's too late for all that, now? Don't you know that? There's no dancing for you. No parties to go to. No new people to see!

GARETH   I don't want that.

GREG   Sarah?

GARETH   I don't want her.

GREG   What do you want?

GARETH   I want to come home. I always… I just want to come home!

GREG   I thought you were going to leave us?

GARETH   Please.

GREG   What do you want?

GARETH   I just want to be left alone!

THEY LET GO OF THE ROPES AND HE FALLS BACK ONTO THE BED.

SMASH TO BLACK.

ABOVE THE SET THE BUTTERFLY FLUTTERS OUT TURNING WILD ARCS BEFORE FALLING INTO BLACKNESS, DEAD.

SCENE 6

THE HOUSE.

IT'S SNOWING.

GARETH IS IN BED, GREG NEXT TO HIM, READING A LETTER.

GARETH   Does she say; "you know".

GREG   She asks after you.

SILENCE.

GREG   (CONT.) You ever go there? Thailand?

GARETH   Short time.

GREG   What's it like, then?

GARETH   Hot. Drugs. Why, you thinking of going?

GREG   What you miss most... you know?

GARETH   Honestly? It's been too long. Women, I suppose, but... I don't know. I've... This's as big as we get. We want it to get bigger we have to actually seek it out. I suppose. But, aye, women, I guess. You?

GREG   Me? No. Not known a lot of women in my life. Not used to it. There was your mother. A couple of girls before that. Not a lot. (PAUSE) Not saying I'm going forever but... I've never seen the world. Perhaps it's my time, like. Anyway. You've got the home and the writing. Sarah tells me I can get it online... the writing. She says I'll be able to read you even over there.

GARETH   Do you even know how to use a computer?

GREG   Someone'll teach me.

GARETH   And you're just going to fuck off and leave me?

GREG   (TIRED) Gareth.

GARETH   For a minute now. You're just going to hand

me over to strangers? That's what's going to happen. To this family!?

GREG   You wanted to go! That's what you said. The home…

GARETH   What if I don't?

GREG   Gareth… you're just scared. That's all. We're all scared. Change is scary. You'll get over it. Anyway, it's booked now.

GARETH   You're just going to fuck off with your bird and leave me rotting on the other side of the world, that it? Fuck would mum have to say about that!

GREG   Your mother…

GARETH   Do you think I killed her, is that it?

GREG   I don't want to do this.

GARETH   Because I do. I think, all the time, that's all I ever get to do and I think; she just couldn't take it anymore. Didn't want to carry one more tray of fucking soup up the fucking stairs anymore and… didn't.

GREG MAKES TO LEAVE.

GARETH   (CONT.) You remember when she died?

GREG STOPS.

GARETH   (CONT.) When the help came. When we had the help. Why would it have been so bad? Just… pills. Pills and water. Pills and water! All those years you could have had!

GREG   It doesn't work like that.

GARETH   This any different?

GREG   You don't really think that.

GARETH   'Sill needs dusting.

ENTER SARAH.

SARAH   You're both here then?

GREG   Sarah.

SARAH   I thought I'd bring some pictures.

(SHE HANDS PHOTOS TO GREG)

SARAH   (CONT.) Of Gareth's new home. (TO GARETH) How you feeling.

GREG   He's not happy about the transition.

SARAH   Who isn't?

GARETH   The passenger.

SARAH   He's got nothing to worry about. He'll be in safe hands. See, that's the view from the outside…

GREG   This is where you work, is it?

SARAH   Me. No. It's nice, isn't it?

GREG   This is his window?

SARAH   One like it. It won't be that exact room of course, but they're all pretty much the same.

GARETH   And you'll be there?

SARAH   It's not about me.

GREG   But you'll look in on him?

SARAH   From time to time, sure. It's not about me. (TO GARETH) It's about you. About your life. It's quality. There'll be plenty of new people to help. Plenty of people to talk to.

GARETH   Just not you.

SARAH   I'm a facilitator. I facilitate. There are lots of people in positions like you. It's my job to make sure they all get the best care. The best life. You wouldn't want to deprive them of that, would you?

GREG   When are you picking him up?

SARAH   An ambulance will be here for him in the morning.

GREG   Not you?

SARAH   I've got an appointment in Milford Haven, I'm afraid. But I'll pop in in a couple of days.

GARETH   I'm a little tired.

SARAH   I thought you'd like to look through some of the testimonials.

GARETH   I'd like to sleep.

SARAH   I'll say goodbye then.

SARAH AND GREG MOVE TO THE TABLE.

SARAH   (CONT.) Change is always going to be hard on him.

GREG   I can go with him?

SARAH   You can. Yes. Though, I'm afraid you won't be able to stay in the home proper. There's a good hotel nearby, one of the nurses'll be able to help you, I'm sure. When's your flight?

GREG   No, I... it wouldn't feel right.

SARAH   He doesn't need you, you know. I know it may look like that, but he doesn't.

GREG   It wouldn't feel right.

SARAH   Suit yourself.

GREG   And that's it, is it? For you?

SARAH   It'll all work out for the best. You'll see. Get on with your life. Let him get on with his. There's just no way this could have worked long term. You do see that, don't you?

GREG   Do you really believe that?

SARAH   Don't you?

GREG   Goodbye, miss.

SARAH   Goodbye Greg. I wish you both the best. I truly do.

GREG   Thank you.

SARAH   We'll be in touch.

GREG NODS A GOODBYE.

EXIT SARAH.

GREG RETURNS TO THE BED.

GARETH   Has she gone.

GREG   Yeah.

GARETH   You know. What I said… about Thailand.

GREG   Drugs not really my thing, like.

GARETH   It's beautiful.

GREG   That right?

GARETH   Right up your street.

GREG   Lovely.

GARETH   We're not actually going anywhere. Right, Dad?

GREG   No. Son. We're not going anywhere.

GARETH   He wouldn't like it. All those strangers' hands.

GREG   No. Me neither, I expect.

GARETH   We'll just stay here.

GREG   Go to sleep.

GREG GETS UP AND FLUFFS THE PILLOWS.

GARETH   Really beautiful.

GREG   Go to sleep now.

GARETH   Do you miss her?

GREG   Who?

GARETH   Mum.

GREG   Very much, lad. Very, very much.

GARETH   Goodnight.

GREG   Sweet dreams.

GARETH GOES TO SLEEP. GREG TAKES A PILLOW AND SMOTHERS HIM.

ANNOUNCER   Flight call 196 to Bangkok. Flight call 196 to Bangkok now boarding. All passengers please make your way to the gate for departure.

THE LIGHTS OF THE BOAT COME UP AND THE SOUND OF THE GHOST BOAT ROCKING ON THE SEA FADES UP AND THEN OUT.

END OF ACT 4.

Thomas Alexander

Also by

DIRECT

LIGHT

Thomas Alexander

THOMAS ALEXANDER

THE VISITOR

BY

THOMAS ALEXANDER

THE VISITOR

WHEN THE LOVER OF A FAMOUS WRITER GOES MISSING IN A WAR RAVAGED COUNTRY HE BRIBES HIS WAY INTO A JAIL TO QUESTION HER HUSBAND, A MISSIONARY, WHO IS BEING TORTURED AS A TRAINING EXERCISE BY HIS CAPTORS.

ALONE IN THE CELL, THE TWO START A DIALOGUE ABOUT THE NATURE OF BELIEF.

BELIEF IN GOD, LOVE, AND POLITICS.

MURDER ME GENTLY

BY

THOMAS ALEXANDER

"ONE MAN... ONE WOMAN... AND THE QUEST FOR JUSTICE IN AN UNJUST WORLD"

MODERN DAY RUSSIA THROUGH THE MEDIUM OF FILM NOIR

BLENDING REAL LIFE EVENTS WITH COMEDY AND INTRIGUE, *MURDER ME GENTLY*'S UNIQUE PERSPECTIVE ON THE WORLD OF RUSSIAN POLITICS AS SEEN THROUGH THE LENS OF FLIM NOIR, SPANS THE ASSASINATION OF INTERNATIONALLY RENOWNED JOURNALISTS, PUTIN'S REACH FOR THE RETURN OF SOVIET SATELITE STATES, AND THE INFLITRATION OF GOVERNMENT BY OLIGARCHS AND CRIMINALS.

PROVIDING A DAMMING INDICTMENT OF THE WEST'S INABILITY TO HALT MOSCOW'S POLICY OF EXPANSIONISM *MURDER ME GENTLY* LENDS A THEATRICAL EXPOSE TO THE VERY REAL WORLD OF CORRUPTION AND GREED IN INTERNATIONAL POLITICS TODAY.

A CONMAN, A DISGRACED INTERPOL AGENT, A MAFIA BOSS, A CIA SPOOK, AND THE SECRET TO THE FUTURE ALL UNITE IN AN UNLIKELY ALLIANCE IN A LOVE AFFAIR THAT WILL DEFINE THE FATE OF THE WORLD IN THOMAS ALEXANDER'S

... MURDER ME ... GENTLY!

93

GREAT

GREAT

BY

THOMAS ALEXANDER

A REMOTE ROOM IN THE THROES OF WINTER.

THE ONCE GREAT MAN LIVES ALONE NOW WITH HIS SON,

AN OLD FRIEND HAS COME TO VISIT. HE HAS CLIMBED UP FROM THE VILLAGE IN ORDER TO OFFER THE OLD MAN ONE LAST CHANCE TO ESCAPE THE ENCROACHING WINTER THAT IS ABOUT TO TAKE HIM, STIRRING UP MEMORIES OF BETTER TIMES AND THE WARMTH OF SUMMER.

BEGAT

BY

THOMAS ALEXANDER

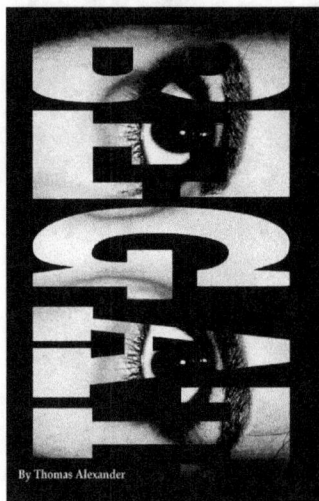

IN A COUNTRY, AFTER THE WAR, A JUDGE THROWS A DINNER PARTY, SEEKING SUPPORT AGAINST A POWERFUL MINISTER WHO HAS RAPED AND KILLED A SERVANT GIRL.

BUT THE JUDGE HIMSELF IS THE TARGET TONIGHT, AND THE SHADOW OF THE WAR HE SO DESPERATELY WANTS TO LEAVE BEHIND THREATENS TO ENGULF HIS FAMILY AS A YOUNG WOMAN SEEKS REVENGE FOR THE SINS OF HIS PAST.

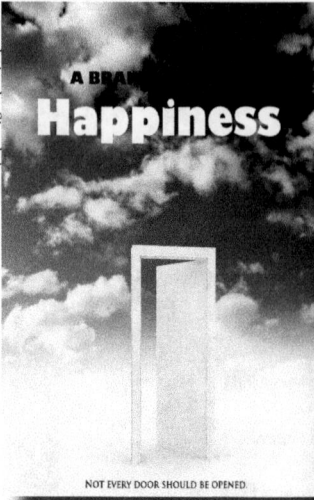

A BRA...
Happiness

NOT EVERY DOOR SHOULD BE OPENED.

HAPPINESS

BY

THOMAS ALEXANDER

ON A REMOTE HEADLAND IN NORTH WALES A MAN AND HIS PARAPLEGIC SON DREAM OF LIFE BEYOND THE CONFINES OF THEIR FOUR WALLS.

BUT WHEN A WOMAN OFFERS THEM THE ESCAPE THEY SO CRAVE THEY FIND THEY ARE BOUND BY MORE THAN THEIR DREAMS.

THE JEALOUSY OF A BORED POLICE-MAN AND THE KINDNESS OF A MAIL ORDER BRIDE SET THEM ON A PATH OF HOPE AND DESTRUCTION.

THE LAST CHRISTMAS

BY

THOMAS ALEXANDER

IT'S NEWS!

WHEN AN EMBATTLED NEWSROOM RECEIVES A POTENTIALLY EARTH SHATTERING STORY MINUTES BEFORE AIR ON CHRISTMAS DAY THE CAREFUL EQUILIBRIUM OF THE TEAM IS SHATTERED AND OLD DIVIDING LINES COME TO THE FORE, TURNING CO-WORKER AGAINST CO-WORKER.

SET IN REAL TIME AND INCORPORATING ACTUAL AND INTERCHANGEABLE NEWS EVENTS THE LAST CHRISTMAS PITS SOCIAL POLITICS AGAINST JOURNALISTIC INTEGRITY IN A BATTLE OF THE ETHICS.

GOD

BY

THOMAS ALEXANDER

WHEN THE NAMED PARTNER OF A SMALL LAW FIRM DIES, LEAVING LARGE DEBT, THE REMAINING MISFITS OF THE FIRM ARE FORCED TO TAKE ON JUST ABOUT ANY CLIENT AVAILABLE, INCLUDING A LITIGIOUS SOCCER-MUM WHO WOULD LIKE TO SUE GOD FOR THE DEATH OF HER HUSBAND – HIT BY A LIGHTNING BOLT ON THE 15TH HOLE OF A MUNICIPAL GOLF COURSE.

THE TRIAL BECOMES COMPLICATED HOWEVER, WHEN AN INDIGENT WITH NO BACKGROUND AND A CANNY KNACK OF KNOWING EVERYONE'S BACKGROUND ENTERS THE COURTROOM CLAIMING TO BE 'GOD'.

BATTING BACK AND FORE BETWEEN THE COURTROOM AND THE PERSONAL LIVES OF THE LAWYERS, 'GOD' IS A FAST PACED COURTROOM DRAMA/COMEDY THAT USES ORIGINAL STAGING AND NON-LINEAR STORYTELLING TO PROVIDE A LIGHTHEARTED, BUT COMPLEX SOCIAL DRAMA.

THE FAMILY

BY

THOMAS ALEXANDER

TODAY, FOR THE FIRST TIME IN LONGER THAN ANYONE CAN REMEMBER, THE FAMILY ARE GATHERING. THEY ARE GATHERING TO CELEBRATE THE ENGAGEMENT OF THE MATRIARCHAL NIECE, THEY ARE GATHERING TO CELEBRATE THE LAST BIRTHDAY OF THE PATRIARCH, THEY ARE GATHERING TO WELCOME HOME THE PRODIGAL SON AND HIS BEAUTIFUL GIRLFRIEND AND THEY ARE GOING TO CELEBRATE ALL THIS WITH A SLIDESHOW.

CANDID PHOTOGRAPHS. PHOTOGRAPHS OF THINGS NO ONE THOUGHT ANYONE ELSE KNEW ABOUT. PHOTOGRAPH TAKEN WHEN NO ONE ELSE WAS THERE.

IT'S ALL COMING OUT TODAY. IN BLACK AND WHITE FOR EVERYONE TO SEE. THE REMNANTS OF CHILD ABUSE, INFIDELITY, LOSS, DESTRUCTION AND MISSED BIRTHDAY PARTIES. IT'S ALL COMING OUT. IT'S GOING TO BE A LONG NIGHT. POSSIBLY FOREVER.

The Recruitment Officer

By

Thomas Alexander

Tom, a charming Yankee recruiter, comes to an unspecified English town and falls in love with the conference centre manager, Julia.

But what exactly is he recruiting for? Why does everyone who joins never come back and what is on the other side of the door

Where do the recruits go after signing up?

An existential love story that asks questions of who we are, what we want from life and whether we're getting it, The Recruitment Officer is a remodelling of the 1706 play by George Farquhar. *The Recruiting Officer*

WRITER'S BLOCK

BY

THOMAS ALEXANDER

PAUL BLOCK WAS ONCE A PROLIFIC WRITER. A RECIPIENT OF BOTH THE PEN AND FAULKNERAWARDS AND THE AUTHOR OF OVER TEN DIFFERENT NOVELS, HE WAS ONCE CONSIDERED THE UK'S MOST UP AND COMING WRITER UNTIL, AT THE AGE OF FORTY, HE SUFFERED A NERVOUS BREAKDOWN.

TEN YEARS LATER THE WORLD HAS FORGOTTEN PAUL BLOCK. HOLED UP IN HIS STUDY HE HAS BEEN WORKING ON THE SAME FIRST PAGE OF HIS NEW NOVEL FOR NEARLY FIVE YEARS, KEPT COMPANY BY ONLY HIS MAID, A FOUL MOUTHED IRISH HIT-MAN, A VETERAN OF THE BATTLE OF GETTYSBURG AND A NINETEEN FORTIES FEMME FATALE.

TODAY, ALL THAT'S GOING TO CHANGE. PAUL HAS A BUSY DAY AHEAD OF HIM. FIRST HE'S GOING TO KILL A PERSISTENT AND CHARMLESS YOUNG REPORTER WHO WANTS TO DO A PIECE ON 'WRITER'S BLOCK' AND THEN HE'S GOING TO HAVE A RARE VISIT FROM HIS SON WHO'S BRINGING HIM BAD NEWS AND A NEW COUCH.

WITH A MISSING BODY AND A SON WHO HATES HIM, PAUL MUST FINALLY RID HIMSELF OF HIS PROTAGONISTS IF HE'S EVER GOING TO STAY OUT OF JAIL, AND FINISH THAT FIRST PAGE.

THOMAS

Japan, 1945 – A Family At War

When a wandering priest escaping a troubled past is taken in by a prominent family, a quiet city in northern Japan is forced to confront the dark shadows of war seeping into their lives in ways they could never have anticipated.

With its townsmen scattered throughout the farthest ends of a desperate empire in a final defence against the encroaching West, the idyllic northern city of Morioka, far removed from the harsh realities of the front, is largely left to itself.

THOMAS ALEXANDER

A Scattering of Orphans

But when a prominent doctor is conscripted and sent to Manila, his sister is left as head of the household and must deal with a young priest living at the bottom of their garden with a large collection of maps and strange knowledge of English.

As the cold hand of war approaches, each person must choose their own destiny and place in the new world.

THE OTHER SIDE

ALEXANDER

Commemorating the 70th Anniversary of the end of WW2! A trilogy spanning the length of the war from the viewpoint of an ordinary Japanese family.

Thomas Alexander

The Disingenuous Martyr

omas Alexander

Beyond The Noonday Sun

Offering a unique perspective through the eyes of a rural Japanese family into the impact of history's bloodiest war to date, *A Scattering of Orphans* is one family's attempt to make sense of a changing world amidst the desolation of war, both home and abroad.

OF THE SUN

THOMAS ALEXANDER

HAPPINESS